EDGE

Katrina Porteous was born in Aberdeen, grew up in Co. Durham, and has lived on the Northumberland coast since 1987. She read History at Cambridge and afterwards studied in the USA on a Harkness Fellowship. Many of the poems in her first collection, *The Lost Music* (Bloodaxe Books, 1996), focus on the Northumbrian fishing community, about which Katrina has also written in prose in *The Bonny Fisher Lad* (The People's History, 2003). Katrina also writes in Northumbrian dialect, and has recorded her long poem, *The Wund an' the Wetter*, on CD with piper Chris Ormston (Iron Press, 1999). Her second full-length collection from Bloodaxe, *Two Countries* (2014), was shortlisted for the Portico Prize for Literature in 2015.

Katrina has been involved in many collaborations with other artists, including public art for Seaham, Co. Durham, with sculptor Michael Johnson, and two books with maritime artist James Dodds, *Longshore Drift* (Jardine Press, 2005) and *The Blue Lonnen* (Jardine Press, 2007). She often performs with musicians, including Chris Ormston, Alistair Anderson and Alexis Bennett. She is particularly known for her radio-poetry, much of it produced by Julian May. One of these poems, *Horse*, with electronic music by Peter Zinovieff, first performed at Sage Gateshead for the BBC Radio 3 Free Thinking Festival 2011, is published as an artists' book and CD, with prints by Olivia Lomenech Gill (Windmillsteads Books, 2014).

Katrina's third full-length collection, *Edge* (Bloodaxe Books, 2019), draws on three collaborations commissioned for performance in Life Science Centre Planetarium, Newcastle, between 2013 and 2016, with multi-channel electronic music by Peter Zinovieff: *Field*, *Sun* and *Edge*. *Sun* was part of NUSTEM's *Imagining the Sun* project for schools and the wider public (Northumbria University, 2016). *Edge*, a poem in four moons incorporating sounds collected from space missions, was broadcast as a *Poetry Please* Special on BBC Radio 4 in 2013.

KATRINA PORTEOUS

EDGE

BLOODAXE BOOKS

Copyright © Katrina Porteous 2019

ISBN: 978 1 78037 490 1

First published 2019 by
Bloodaxe Books Ltd,
Eastburn,
South Park,
Hexham,
Northumberland NE46 1BS.

www.bloodaxebooks.com
For further information about Bloodaxe titles
please visit our website and join our mailing list
or write to the above address for a catalogue.

Supported by
**ARTS COUNCIL
ENGLAND**

Cover design: Neil Astley & Pamela Robertson-Pearce.

Printed in Great Britain by Bell & Bain Limited, Glasgow, Scotland, on
acid-free paper sourced from mills with FSC chain of custody certification.

For all my teachers

CONTENTS

INTRODUCTION

I

Why does the Sun shine? Why do stars, planets, galaxies, human beings – or any matter – exist at all? What is time? Variations on these questions have concerned poets for millennia. They have been, for thousands of years, questions of theology. In our own time, science is providing astonishing answers. What could be more inspirational to a poet? To anyone?

When I was at school, nearly half a century ago, I chose to study Arts rather than Sciences. Now I am trying to make up for that deficit, by working alongside research scientists, to ask them naive questions and translate what they have discovered to a general readership. So this is a book of collaborations; not so much about science, as a poet's view of science and the poetry of science, an imaginative narrative of how things came to be the way they are, through an increasing complexity of organisation: from physics to chemistry and – eventually – to biology. As well as translation, it is a book of interrogation, of aesthetics and wonder; a search for alternative narratives to replace old theologies – a book with almost no people in it, that explores landscapes of other worlds, mapping the particular place of Earth, life and human consciousness against the unimaginable scales of nature. It is at once a celebration of the miracle of being alive, and an attempt to create a less anthropocentric poetry of nature.

I live by the sea, and the 300-million-year-old Carboniferous rocky foreshore reminds me daily that human existence – perhaps around half a million years old, depending on how you define human – is only a blink of the eye in the history of our four-and-a-half-billion-year-old planet. Each month, I watch the full Moon rise over the waves. I am reminded anew of the ubiquity of wave-forms in nature, of the sheer strangeness of life on Earth, and of the cold emptiness of outer space. Since the epoch when the rocks I see from my window were laid down, there have been at least three mass extinctions. Whatever the role and future of our species, it appears that we are currently in the midst of another.

The collaborations which gave rise to these poems were not only with research scientists: in each case I worked closely with the inspirational electronic composer, inventor and polymath Peter Zinovieff. The book is based on three performance-pieces which we created together for Life Science Centre Planetarium in Newcastle between 2013 and 2016. Each piece is very different from the others – that was one of our aims – but all share features in common. Each lasts for 25 to 30 minutes, and the text of each was written to be performed live as a continuous whole with Peter's multi-channel music. In each performance, the words are carefully timed to the music, and become part of it. At these events, the work is introduced by a scientist, who gives a short talk on the subject; and each performance is accompanied by stunning visual images – real photographs drawn from space and terrestrial telescopes, rendered for the planetarium dome by Christopher Hudson and for flat screen by Stephen Patterson (*Edge*) and Jonathan Sanderson (*Sun*).

The experience of these live performances is very different from reading text on the page. Each introductory science talk provides background for understanding the text, the text interacts constantly with the music, the visual images act as signposts to the landscape to which text and music refer, and the whole experience is, in the current expression, "immersive". Nevertheless, each text began as a series of individual poems, and the sequences are presented here as such. They are intended for an audience with no scientific knowledge, and for the words to stand on their own. Within each sequence, I have given each poem a title, to replace the visual clues in the performance, and so make the text more accessible to the reader.

The book is divided into three parts. Part I, *Field*, deals with the strange quantum worlds underlying the Universe. In particular it concentrates on the long-theorised and recently verified Higgs field, without which matter could not exist. Part II, *Sun*, moves from the micro to the macro, focusing on the star at the centre of our local solar system, its physical structures and processes, upon which that system – and light, warmth and the miraculous development of life on Earth – depend. Part III, *Edge*, takes us on a journey to four different worlds – four moons of the solar system, whose differences are taken in the poem to represent the ancient "primary elements" of Fire, Water, Earth and Air. *Edge* ends with Earth's own Moon, a familiar yet entirely dead world, which paradoxically plays a vital role in the emergence and continuance of life on Earth. Each of these sequences is framed by a few short poems, con-ceived at the same time, but not included in the planetarium performances. The book ends with a Coda of three poems from planet Earth.

How does a poet with no background in science approach astronomy, cosmology and particle physics? To begin, I read widely in popular science. Important texts for me were *The Particle at the End of the Universe* by Sean Carroll, Roger Pen-rose's magnificent *The Road To Reality*, Leon Golub and Jay Pasachoff's *Nearest Star* and Lucie Green's *15 Million Degrees*. Secondly, I found the visual imagery widely available on the web from spacecraft – such as the NASA/ESA Hubble Space Telescope and Solar and Heliospheric Observatory (SOHO) and NASA's newer Solar Dynamics Observatory (SDO) – immensely inspiring. So too were the astonishing photographs taken on space missions such as NASA's Galileo and NASA/ESA's Cassini-Huygens. I spent many hours poring over collections of space photographs, such as Michael Benson's *Beyond: A Solar System Voyage*.

Although there is no sound in space, a third source of inspir-ation was the raw sound on which Peter based his music: sounds from various space missions, and sounds derived from solar oscillation data. Lastly, and most importantly, I was fortunate to enjoy scientific support, not just from Life Planetarium but from two universities: from Professor Tom Lancaster, Department of Physics, Durham University (for *Field*), and from Northumbria University's Solar Physics Research Group and NUSTEM (for *Sun*, part of the STFC-funded *Imagining the Sun* project). For each of these pieces I did try to learn some basic physics. Even so, after several months' immersion in each subject, I realised that, without the language of mathematics, I could know almost nothing; only enough to ask naive questions, as I would encourage anyone to do.

So these poems have an epistemological element: they are not just about *what* we know, but about *how* we know. The relation between scientific empiricism and poetic idealism fascinates me. In each case, I found myself writing my way towards a crude understanding of the subject, just as I would if I was grappling with a difficult human experience. The struggle to understand was also the effort to forge a language in which to interrogate the subject. Since understanding was never more than proximate, the aim of each piece is not to convey accurate scientific information, but rather to translate the experience of trying to understand. As in any poem, my intention is not to explain anything, only to evoke some things. Much of this is achieved through metaphor, and through the physicality of sound.

I hope that these poems will at least open up some questions to a non-scientific audience. To facilitate this, it might be helpful to say a little more about how each piece came into being.

II

My collaboration with Peter Zinovieff began in 2011 with *Horse*, a piece for BBC Radio 3's *Between the Ears*. *Horse* dealt with deep time, geological, mythological and historical. Our work with the planetarium followed in 2013 with *Edge*, the last piece in this book. The immediate stimulus was a proposed *Earth Music* festival for radio, which, although it did not materialise, gave us the impetus to submit an idea, make contact with the planetarium, and receive a generous invitation from Life Science Centre to begin work.

The poems are not presented here in the order in which they were written, but rather in an order which makes sense as a narrative – from the beginning of the Universe to the creation of conscious life. *Field*, the first sequence in the book, was written in 2015 and premiered at *Maker Faire*, an international science and creativity gathering, at Life Science Centre in April that year. It was our second planetarium piece. The idea to write about quantum fields was Peter's. Following our exploration of the solar system in *Edge*, the subject appealed to my naive curiosity. Since adolescence, I have felt drawn to theoretical physics, without having any real understanding of it. This was my chance to ask questions. In 2012, two teams working at CERN's Large Hadron Collider in Switzerland had confirmed the Standard Model of particle physics, which tells us that all reality is constructed from a small number of fundamental particles. They had done so by providing observational proof of the existence of the Higgs boson, the last missing piece of the model.

The discovery of the Higgs was an amazing moment, because it supplied actual empirical evidence of what the mathematical theory had suggested for many years. The Higgs provides the mechanism which gives all matter its mass. Without mass, there would be no gravitational attraction, and therefore no stars, planets or galaxies. The theory behind the Higgs was mathematically predicted by a number of scientists, among them Newcastle-born Peter Higgs, who gave it its name. So it has for me a specific local connection. At the same time, my imagination is fired by the thought of the Large Hadron Collider, the biggest machine ever built, which is used to explore the smallest building-blocks of matter. I find the imagination and creativity of this invention incredibly exciting.

Theoretical physics raises endless questions. By recreating the conditions of the very early Universe, the LHC could provide some answers and further leads. For example, the theory suggests that the symmetries of the Standard Model may be part of a greater "supersymmetry". Cosmology also indicates that the Universe is largely composed of mass which we cannot see (dark matter) and that it is expanding at an ever-faster rate (dark energy). The LHC could provide proof for these theories. These are the most exciting developments in our knowledge of the Universe and our place in it. I wanted to capture some of that excitement in *Field*.

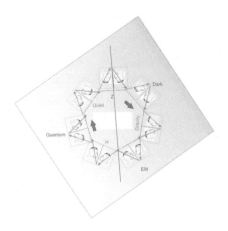

Peter began the creative process by drawing a structure (above). He suggested that our piece should have seven movements, and that the music of each movement should contain a symmetry. Symmetry is a key idea underlying quantum field theory. The Higgs, which makes reality possible, breaks an initial symmetry of the Universe. We considered seven a good number because it gives our piece an asymmetric shape.

Peter lives in Cambridge and I live in Northumberland, so most of our collaboration has been electronic. We wrote the music and words for each piece in parallel. Peter's music for *Field* includes a theme played on real instruments, which continually recurs, and represents the Higgs field constituting the background to all reality. Each of the movements is divided between a section of music with words, and a section of music without.

We selected photographic images for *Field* from the Hubble Space Telescope. Many of these show light from stars in the early Universe at wavelengths far beyond human senses. Others show clouds of dust and gas from which stars are formed. These real images from the distant cosmos show the large-scale effects of very small quantum processes. They illustrate the way mass (the result of the Higgs) causes gravity to bend space and time. No one knows exactly how quantum theory fits with our large-scale Universe. That is the great unanswered question, which *Field* also addresses.

To me, the most amazing thing about physics is its beauty – of which I shall say more later. Like most non-scientists, however,

I struggle with the mathematical and technical languages which make science seem so alien. In writing *Field*, I deliberately avoided using science terms like quarks, fermions and bosons, which many people might not understand. Instead, I use metaphor. Some of the themes of *Field* are surprisingly simple. For example, the symmetries which underlie reality are not unlike the "Ideas" of the ancient Greek philosopher, Plato. The fact that symmetries are broken in our Universe (by the Higgs) reminds me of Plato's belief that we cannot see true reality, only its partial image. The reader does need to know any science to grasp these basic ideas.

Shortly after the premiere of *Field*, Northumbria University's NUSTEM team announced a project called *Imagining the Sun*. This involved a visual artist, Helen Schell, and work with a number of schools on Tyneside. It gave Peter and me the opportunity to extend our collaboration, with our third planetarium piece, *Sun* – an artistic response to the work of Northumbria University's Solar Physics research group. How do we investigate the Sun when it is so dangerous to look at it directly? In the first half of 2016 I met the solar scientists, read all I could about the Sun, studied videos and still images from NASA's Solar Dynamics Observatory and other solar telescopes, and once again tried, through the process of writing, to get to grips with what I learnt. The result was a series of about 20 poems.

I shared some of this work with the solar physicists in a seminar, and their responses caused me again to reflect on how differently scientists and poets use language. Poets "evoke" atmosphere through rhythm, word-music and imagery, whereas scientists are traditionally said to use language "objectively" – not to evoke but to signpost or "signify". Yet talking to solar scientists, I discovered fascinating personal differences in the way that they conceive of the Sun. Some argued that it should be depicted as quiet, serene and benevolent, others, as dynamic, violent and explosive. Of course, these contradictory points of view are both simultaneously true. Everything depends upon perspective: every scientific model, every hypothesis. To that extent, science too involves story-telling.

Once again, my collaboration with Peter on *Sun* took place mostly at a distance. In this case, Peter's electronic music for six separate tracks, written in four movements, was entirely derived from oscillation data from an instrument on the SOHO space-craft, the Michelson Doppler Imager. Each movement represents a five-minute solar cycle. SOHO's solar sounds, available on the Stanford University website, are a fantastic stimulus to the imagination. So are visual images like the SOHO sunquakes signature, and images from newer solar telescopes like SDO. At the same time, these sounds and images raise questions. Is it sound if it must be speeded up 42,000 times to be audible? What do scientists mean when they say that they use sound to "look" inside the Sun?

SUN

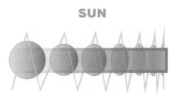

First, Peter sent me this drawing to represent the structure of our piece. Then, as the shape and texture of his music emerged, he began to send sound files, and I selected and organised 17 of the original poems which I felt would work with them to explore questions posed by solar physics. Once we had our structure and exact timings for the music and text, I worked again with Chris Hudson, who produced awe-inspiring full-dome visuals. We used these partly to illustrate or illuminate the text and music, and more importantly to create atmospheres to lead the audience on a journey where their own senses could not take them.

Working together, the poetry, music and images explore the physical structure and processes of the Sun, revealed in wave-lengths beyond human perception: how its magnetic fields are generated, how sunquakes occur, and the ways in which sound is used to peer inside it. Little by little, the music, words and visuals strip the layers of our nearest star, allowing us to travel where the body cannot, to experience a reality not otherwise accessible to sight or hearing.

Writing *Sun* deepened my awe and wonder at the natural world: that life on Earth is only made possible by the Sun; that it is only through an almost miraculous convergence of factors that human life has evolved; that we are protected from the damaging "solar wind" of cosmic rays by Earth's magnetic field, and from our star's UV radiation by Earth's filtering atmosphere; and that, ultimately, everything that has ever existed is made out of stardust. All simple elements are manufactured in stars, and heavier elements only develop as stars evolve from birth to death and their material is recycled to form new generations of stars. I find these facts astonishing, and endlessly inspiring.

Edge, the last of the three poem sequences in this collection, was the earliest of our planetarium pieces. I have placed it last in this book because it deals with the most evolved physical land-scapes – also in some ways the most familiar. *Edge* is different in atmosphere from the preceding sequences. As with the others, the text was arranged in response to the structure of Peter's music; but in this case his instructions and timings were especially precise. As a result, this text is more closely adapted to its music than the others.

Edge takes us on a sound-journey to four different worlds – four moons of our solar system representing what the Ancients believed to be the primary elements, Fire, Water, Earth and Air. They are Jupiter's fiery moon Io; two of Saturn's moons, icy Enceladus and methane-rich Titan; and Earth's own Moon. Enceladus, with its subterranean ocean of salty liquid water, is exciting because scientists believe that it may meet many of the conditions needed for primitive Earth-like life to evolve. Saturn's giant moon Titan, with its methane lakes and hydrocarbon atmosphere, has a strange, cold chemistry which could possibly provide a basis for truly alien life. Jupiter's moon Io, violently volcanic, represents an entirely hostile, dynamic world which continually remakes itself. The fourth world, our own Moon, is a dead world, which paradoxically plays a vital role in the mira-culous emergence and continuance of life on Earth.

Peter's computer music for *Edge* incorporates sound data from space missions – Sputnik, Apollo and Voyager, and the landing of the Cassini mission's Huygens probe on Titan. As with the other pieces, the music was written simultaneously with the text over several months; each developed in response to the other, following Peter's precise initial structure. For this piece, he suggested a tidal form, which has its origins in Act 3 of his libretto for Sir Harrison Birtwistle's opera, *The Mask of Orpheus* (1986):

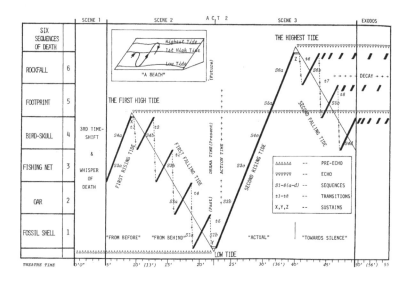

Sir Harrison Birtwistle 'The Mask of Orpheus | Opera in 3 acts'
Libretto and scenario by Peter Zinovieff
© Copyright 1986 by Universal Edition (London) Ltd, London/UE17683

The structure of rising and falling tides allows the audience to visit and revisit each world in turn, experiencing, as they do so, a relation between chaos and cosmos. Along the way are strewn clues to the possibility of the first stirrings of primitive life. Finally, from Earth's Moon, we catch sight of our own planet, distinguished by the emergence not only of self-replicating life, in the form of molecules of DNA, but ultimately of complex consciousness and imagination. In the end, although the piece takes the listener to entirely non-human worlds, *Edge* is about what it means to be human, to have imagination, in space and time.

Edge was written with support from Arts Council England Grants for the Arts. It was recorded in front of an audience in

Life Science Centre Planetarium during the British Science Festival in September 2013, and broadcast on BBC Radio 4 as a *Poetry Please* Special, performed by me with actor David Seddon, and produced by Julian May. The simultaneous layering of voices in the radio performance is replicated on the page by double columns of text.

I was delighted to have the opportunity to bring *Edge* to a national radio audience; but concluded that, in spite of Julian's magnificent efforts, radio was not the right medium for the piece. The poem draws on a wide range of dramatic voices – whispers, shouts, chants and incantations. Peter's music was written for six-channel surround sound, not for stereo. When we stage the piece live, as we have in a variety of venues, the drama of the performance, music and images together – loud, and at times overwhelming – immerses the audience in an experience which is almost the opposite of the intimate space of radio. In addition, although Peter's music provides very clear markers, with a different theme for each moon, the complex tidal structure of *Edge* is easier to follow with the sequence of real space photographs which is part of each performance. The text presented here replaces these musical and visual clues with titles, which identify the location of each scene.

III

Although *Edge* is the last part of the book, it was the beginning of an adventure for me. It explored themes which have long concerned me in my work – landscape, nature and time. *Field* enabled me to investigate these themes in a more abstract sense, and *Sun* to examine the application of certain quantum processes on a cosmic scale. Scale and perspective are central themes throughout this book.

My own sense of aesthetic or "spiritual" reality underwent an evolution in the course of writing this work. Creating *Edge*, which concentrates on the cold immensities of space, visiting hostile landscapes utterly devoid of human warmth, was a bleak and terrifying experience. *Field*, however, had the opposite effect on me: I found the sheer beauty of the symmetry transformations within the equations immensely moving. They touched me like music or great architecture. As a poet, I would call that aesthetic experience spiritual. Some scientists would not agree with that description, but every scientist would know what I mean. I hope that *Field* will give everyone some access to that beauty.

Writing these pieces has left me with a number of observations. First is the recognition that, as T.S. Eliot said in a different context, 'humankind cannot bear very much reality'; or, to put it another way, reality is quite different from what we perceive it to be. Our anthropocentric language is wholly inadequate to describe it. Our senses have evolved to interpret the part of the available data on this planet that our ancestors found useful to survive. But "sound" is only one way of experiencing a mechanical wave of pressure and displacement. And "light" is only part of a vast spectrum of electromagnetic energy, of which, like the inhabitants of Plato's cave, we only see a tiny slice. Science enables us to build machines which extend our senses to observe a greater or deeper reality – space telescopes like SDO, which photographs in 10 wavelengths, allowing us to see what we could never otherwise perceive, or vast microscopes, the biggest of which is the Large Hadron Collider. How astonishing our species is, to imagine and achieve this.

Yet, if we are to translate science from mathematics into words, we still need narrative. Quantum theory demands a moment of perfect symmetry which, for matter to exist, must be broken; and beyond which, despite that breaking, the symmetries persist. In this, one might detect echoes of ancient narratives; Platonic forms, perhaps, or a Judeo-Christian structure of fall and redemption. So my second recognition concerns the ways in which certain narratives, metaphors and philosophical structures of Western thought continue to resonate with contemporary scientific theory and discovery. Indeed, I would argue that to describe the world using words rather than mathematical language is inevitably to resort to metaphor.

Third is a linguistic point: the inescapable – probably irresolvable – tension between the precision of scientific technical language and the (different) precision and integrity of poetic language. Several words or metaphors which my science advisors challenged in poems I had in the end to leave in place: the imagery of mirrors, for example. There is an inevitable clash here. I worked hard to try to understand the physics; and I tried to push the language to describe it more accurately; but the tension between accuracy and the kind of generative internal energy required by a poem (the various "fields" of language and the interactions between them) at times overwhelm the signing function of technical language. There may be families of images within a poem sequence, particular allusions which relate to one another subtly within and across the poems; and allowing the integrity of these may be at odds with what the signing function demands.

Exactly the same is true of the musical qualities of language (which further relate to Peter's music). The poem's internal soundscape requires certain things which the specifically technical language will not allow. When I speak of the "fields" of language, what I mean is this: a poem holds within it a simultaneity, multi-dimensionality, the interplay between its sounds, structure, imagery and meaning. Unlike informational prose, a poem cannot be read in a linear way. When I write a poem I am listening to the resonances between all these elements, and am guided by them; while always trying also to remain true to some external reality. In the case of these sequences, that external reality is more than usually demanding, because it also has an objective, mathematical description, which most poetic subjects do not. So this has been a particularly interesting and exacting challenge for me. In fact, life-changing.

ACKNOWLEDGEMENTS

For the poems that make up the three performance pieces in this book many thanks are due. Each piece is a collaboration. I am particularly grateful to Life Science Centre at the International Centre for Life, Newcastle, for their support. Former Science Communications Director Ian Simmons invited Peter and me to create the pieces, and Head of Special Projects Andy Lloyd sparked the initial interest. Thanks to them, and to all the fantastic team at Life, particularly Planetarium Supervisor Christopher Hudson, for his long shifts programming the visual elements. Special thanks to Head of Public Engagement, Elin Roberts, who kept each show on the road at some anxious moments.

For *Field*, I am grateful to the Society of Authors for an Authors' Foundation Award, which bought me time to write. Thanks to Professor Jon Butterworth, University College London, Dr Robert Appleby, University of Manchester, and Dr Marieke Navin, Science and Industry Museum, Manchester, for their input. Particular thanks to Professor Tom Lancaster at Durham University Department of Physics for generously giving his time for our inspirational discussions.

For *Sun*, thanks to the Science and Technology Facilities Council for financial support for *Imagining the Sun*, and to Professor John Woodward, Faculty Pro Vice-Chancellor, Engineering and Environment, Northumbria University, for engaging us. Thanks to all the Northumbria University solar physicists who gave their time to the piece, especially Professor James McLaughlin and Dr Richard Morton. Special thanks to Professor Valentina Zharkova for her initial input and her responses. Thanks to my brilliant colleague, visual artist Helen Schell, and to all the outstanding team at NUSTEM for the success of *Imagining the Sun*; to Dr Sarah Hilton (now at Durham University) for editing the project booklet, and to Jonathan Sanderson for making an online version of *Sun*. Particular thanks to Dr Carol Davenport, Director of NUSTEM, for her inestimable work coordinating and supporting the project throughout.

For *Edge*, thanks to Sarah Blunt at the BBC Natural History Unit for her initial encouragement, to Arts Council England Grants for the Arts for financial support, to Stephen 'Stig' Patterson for his fantastic technical expertise, and to Universal Edition (London) Ltd for permission to use the image on page 18. I am especially grateful to Julian May at BBC Radio 4 for his herculean efforts to get the piece on air.

The science writers and communicators who have informed these poems are too many to thank individually. They include all the writers mentioned in my introduction, and broadcasters, notably Professor Brian Cox and the team involved in producing his many BBC television series, who help make astronomy accessible to people like me. I am especially indebted to all the international scientists involved in past and present missions to investigate these worlds. They include scientists from the NASA Apollo programme, NASA's Voyager I and II, Galileo and SDO, and the NASA/ESA Hubble Space Telescope, Cassini-Huygens mission and SOHO, as well as all those working on other terrestrial and space telescopes, and at the Large Hadron Collider, CERN. They are the great explorers of our age.

All three planetarium pieces have been adapted for flat screen and stereo delivery, and I have performed them in a variety of venues. Thanks to VARC (Highgreen) and artist Helen Pailing, *Edge* was heard in Tarset village hall, Northumberland, as part of Dark Skies with a Woolly Twist (2014). I also performed it at New Networks for Nature (Stamford Arts Centre, Lincolnshire, 2014). I performed part of *Field* at Deranged Poetesses (Apples and Snakes, ARC Theatre, Stockton, 2019). I performed *Sun* in 2017 at the Sound and Environment conference, University of Hull, at Sounding Out the Space, Dublin Institute of Technology, and at Poetry-next-the-Sea, Norfolk. In 2018 I performed it at Durham Festival of the Arts. I also performed excerpts in 2017 at Words by the Water, Keswick, at the BIG Event STEM Communicators' Conference, Newcastle, at Berwick Literary Festival, and widely in schools. I am grateful to Dr Helen Mason, Reader in Solar Physics at the Department of Applied Mathematics and Theoretical Physics, University of

Cambridge, for supporting *Sun*.

Some of these poems have appeared in print in the following publications: *Follow the Sun*, ed. Keith Armstrong (Northern Voices, 2016); *Imagining the Sun* (Northumbria University NUSTEM, 2017); *Temenos* (Windmillsteads Books, 2017); *Woven Landscapes* (Avalanche, 2017); *Front Court* (Trinity Hall Newsletter, Spring 2018); and *Word Sharing* (Tübingen University and Tübingen Cultural Office, 2018). Additional thanks to Trinity Hall, Cambridge and the Poetry School for commissioning *Wake* as part of THwomen40 and the Poetry School's 20th anniversary Pavement Poetry. In November 2017 the poem was stencilled on the college Front Court pavement in "smart" materials which showed up when it rained.

Special thanks to the following friends, colleagues and family for their encouragement: to Harry Beamish, Martin Pacey, and Mary and Stuart Manley at Barter Books, Alnwick; to Dr Keith Armstrong for suggesting Life Science Centre as a possible venue; to Dr Pete Edwards, Director of Science Outreach, Durham University; to Neil Astley and all at Bloodaxe Books for their commitment to my work; to Peter's wife Jenny Zinovieff; and most of all to Peter Zinovieff, not only for his astonishing musical collaboration but for many years of inspiration. Without him, these poems would never have been written. Finally, to my mother and father, Joan and Ian Porteous, my heartfelt thanks for their love and support always.

I

Volcanoes of Io

You thought you knew
What matter was.
Solid or gas

Or fluid. These words
And their slippery properties –
Speed. Heat. Light. Mass –

One seething molten
Caldera, spitting gobs
That cool on the surface

Into gleaming, desirable
Pennies, rolling
Back into the furnace

Like the old gods
Slipping off their bodies
Out of mischief, or pity.

FIELD

Field

I

They will not mesh, the very small and the large.
They will not converge.

On that side of the mirror, flickering fringes –
Superposition, quantum probabilities,
Shimmering light and dark; on this,

Nature has made its choice.
Time, space –
They will not bend both ways at once.

When the little ideas slip into their bodies like clothes
They step through the mirror, enter
An irreducible level of noise –

Gravitational decoherence, dependent on mass.

Worlds, how sad we are to leave our dreaming behind.
So lovely we were then, so light, so playful.

But how compelling to have a body. In fact,

Irresistible.

Quiet

I

Zero
Could bear its own company
Not a zeptosecond longer. Abrupt

Disjuncture. One moment
An undifferentiated plane –
Heat, sheer as water.

The next, everywhere
Glittering crystalline.

And Zero alone knows
Why this has happened:
Why it has smashed itself

To see what lies inside the mirror.

Quiet

II

Tell it again.
You might have known
It would begin with violation.

Inconceivably hot
Cooled
Unspeakably fast.

Something froze out –

Fluency, locking to ice.
Some spontaneous

Crack.

Weak interactions
Making their fateful choice.

And all because something
Is lurking in the background.

Some old instigator,
Sneaking among the maidens.

This
Gaining mass
By gobbling up That.

The Ancients were right. It is all
Coupling
And disguises,

Feverishly swapping bodies
When no one is looking.

Gravity

I

Then the deep past
Enters experience
From the outside, enormous.

Face to face
With the thing that made it,
Experience cannot take it in.

One by one, the heavens
Compose their questions.
Structure. Order. Shape.

What is your particle?
Where is your opposite?
Some dark energy

Forcing space apart.
Some folded secret.
All those missing pieces.

Gravity

II *(after Miroslav Holub)*

Here, too, the peaks and valleys,
Planets, moons, stars
Rolling, helpless, in rivers.

Here, too, the circle dance,
The soundless music
Writing its order in deep space.

A map of all possible relations.
Tendencies towards or away from.
Here, too, the familiar geographies –

Stretching, pushing out
On something pressing back.
The embattled stars'

Eventual collapse.
The madly-spinning Catherine-wheel's
Demonic pulse.

Here, too, the roaring falls.
Oblivion. The river
Tearing faster and faster.

Electromagnetism

I *Gauge Theory*

What are the symmetries doing today?

They don't care where you are.
They are dispassionate in their procedure.
It is excellent that we can rely on the symmetries –

Their global force, their implacable machinery.
We hear a rumour that their operations
Sanction the actual only provincially.

What if the symmetries were to fail us?

We only exist by permission of the symmetries –
As we speed into element and chemistry, we beg them
That they might continue to permit us to dwell

Momentarily within their parentheses.

Electromagnetism

II

If there is a beginning
This is its signature.
Its first scribble.

Not a continuum.
Only the sum
Of countless discrete

Shivers, a meaningless
Cipher that becomes
Gas, dust, and at least

One exquisite accident –
An instrument
To interpret its imprint.

Astonishing that, across
Immense distance,
It should speak,

Cold and articulate
As zigzags of light.
And if an infant

Cannot translate –
Cannot receive
Its message –

Still, it is born
Hard-wired, of the one
Unnegotiable grammar.

Higgs

I

At a stroke
Everywhere is instantly
Indelibly local.

When the numbers' austere
Machinery shatters,
The shimmering little ideas

Snap into the actual.
Look –
They are dancing together.

Down the mirrored corridor
An echo of laughter.

Higgs

II

Be slippery, be everywhere never the same,
Be the invisible crowd in the boundless room
We push-me-pull through, everywhere never be seen,

Be handicap, be hindrance, be small impediment,
Be brake, be check, be drogue, be spider-web, be sticking-point,
Be none of these.
Be either

A glimpse of a greater symmetrical structure,
Dilating, flowering out of a centre,
A grander rose window, a brilliance branching
Into the dark, its relic abundance;

Or be accidental, a function of chance,
Occurring just here, only once,
In a film of space
Curled between this universe and the next

And the next, in a randomness so immense,
Its froth – its endless bubbling numbers,
Universes winking and vanishing –
Will not compute.

Just be one or the other.

Quantum

I

Spin
Was symmetry's idea.
It bartered with space.

How will it become
Tangible substance?
How will it translate

Its quantities into perceptible force,
Into matter?

A ladder,
Stepping momentum in packages.

Strange transformations.

Identical particles,
Swapping identities.
One thought, two faces.

These: flipped to a minus-sign,
Keep one another out.
Here I am – substance.

These: changed without changing,
Stack up in heaps.
Pass it on – force.

And this, a disturbance
In something that is everywhere

And always not nothing, its spin
Zero, the point
That bestows mass,

Whatever
The frame of reference.

Quantum

II

Emptiness, you are a paradox.
You are not empty.
You are full of numbers.

Wherever you are, expect commerce.
Matter travelling through you
Slows to do business.

Emptiness, you are a marketplace.
Matter, you are trade.

Only the light escapes
Free, gratis,
And the thing that holds us together.

Dark

The symmetries interrogate their provinces.
One particular plane.

Where has it gone –
Your dark mass? Your invisible particle?
Questions of scale.

Shoals of galaxies, rushing apart,
Light of the farthest
Bent like a question-mark.

What is your geometry, your smallest resolution?
What hidden relation
Resolves its shimmering into the actual?

Questions of perspective.
How a point propagates,
Blossoms, becomes a string, a sheet, a brane.

So much is missing,

Unknown to itself, its own secret syntax,
Slippery, amnesiac, able to entertain
Many thoughts at a time.

Field

II

When the little ideas entered mass
Everything fell into place.

Those ethereal nothings snapped into their bodies midflight.

Actuality. Structure and pattern,
Time, space, anyworld, unfolding –

Excellent to be dark and undetectable,
Brilliant to be matter and its opposite –

Everything manifold, possible, all of it becoming.

So it has been ever since that bright mirror broke.
One side, everything floats.

All matter dreams of being nothing but light.

II

Various Uncertainties

I

Forget harmony. Forget
Chemistry – this
Singing together with that.

Forget melody. Forget
Stretched space, stars swept
Into its crook.

Roll back the clock.
It is a question of scale.
How close can you get?

One note, elastic
To the utmost. Countless
Shivers of excitement.

Aurora

Sometimes in the high latitudes
The whole night
Writhes in its prison.

Green sheets thrash
And twist in an unknown
Wind, wild rivers

Making for elsewhere
In the dark. Particle,
Wave, in ever-changing

Torrents, caged
And volatile, the invisible
Meeting itself in disguise,

Arrives, alight,
To remind Earth of its own
Incalculable strangeness.

Observatory

Suddenly the Sun turns green.
Pixel by pixel
It is surrendering its secrets.

Something peers up at it
Through a pin-prick, a peep-hole.
Maybe from a prison, a cave, maybe a shelter.

The green Sun nakedly submits
To interrogation. Furious,
Delicate. Peeled. It rips,

Slits, tears itself endlessly, stripping
Its chiffons, its gauzes,
Layer after layer, indigo, violet –

Chromosphere, quiet corona, hot flare plasma.
Filaments, loops,
Firing back intelligence.

Experience
Cannot be sure of itself. Who
Is interrogating whom? The answer

Escapes like black light. Truth
Is a burning thing, imaged
In many wavelengths.

SUN

Real

Darkness said to the Sun
Who are you?
That quiet, pale face.

Grainy greyscale newspaper photo –
I want to know your bones.

Strip you. Skin,
Tissues. Like a scalpel.

As many faces
As there are wavelengths to tune into.

Is it temperature, is it weather,
Where does it begin and end,

Those dark moods, hidden
Outbursts, broadcast to no one?

I want to plumb

How they mutter to each other,
Your inside-outside

Singing to itself, your underworld,
Your echogram, your sonar,

Your heartbeat, your brain-scan,
Your every last secret.

Which is the real Sun?

All of them.

None.

Dynamo

Imagine a thing with two hearts,

A slow, formal dance
Taking place inside it.
Intimate

And alike, two pairs of dancers
Slowly moving closer, step
By step, heartbeat by heartbeat.

Everything they touch
Is profoundly moved.

But slowly
The moment passes. It cycles
Differently each time.

Soon, they will mirror each other
Exactly, two pairs
Out of sync, and far

Apart in their separate
Hemispheres. But still

Quietly intimate.

Hydrostatic Equilibrium

Long and slow. Long, long and slow.

At perfectly
Regular intervals, a strangeness
Heaves and sighs.

Something tremendous
Hoiking it together.

Something enormous
Shoving it apart.

Spin, twist, heap, drag, squeeze
Becoming
Temperature, mass, radiance, luminosity –

This deeper dance
In which all hold hands in a ferocious

Motion, which is also absolutely
Exquisite

Balance.

Rotation Patterns

Long and slow. Long, long and slow.
Again and again
Adventurers, ranks of soldiers,

Dive in from the rippling surface,
Sample the flow
At various levels; are spun

Faster near the equator,
Slower near the poles –
Explore lower and deeper

To the crucible of difference
Beyond which some solid
Spins as a whole.

Back where it began, the visible
Tells tales on the invisible –
Is it a clue? A sign? Is it a signal?

The auguries
Cry out for their interpreters:

Something gathering
On the far side of the Sun.

Sunquake

Who is bouncing pebbles on the Sun's slow drum?

Is it temperature, is it density, can you hear it

Repeatedly signing its name
With a hammer in ripples in fire, in dark rings?

Something from high, high up, a thought
Recurring
At differing intervals,

Talking to itself in the body's secret deep cavities.

Does it leave a trace?
Does it make a noise?

Where has it been?

Sunspots

What are these dark wounds
Wheeling, gathering?
What do they say?

Do they disclose their sources,
Will they inform, will they
Blab, will they spill, will they squeal on Stretch

And Snap, twisting inside?
Will they testify?
How will they betray

Inside to outside? Who listens? Who reads
Their intelligence? When
Their invisible ink

Fills up with light and their brilliant arcs
Touch – Flash – will they report
Back to their sources, be seen,

Heard, through the din,
Through the hammering factories, trapped
In pipe and drum?

Many

How do they talk to each other, its too-many faces,
Eleven-year cycles, five-minute oscillations,

Pockmarked orange-peel granulations,
Its jam-pan, its whirlpools flowering and fading?

What have they to say to one another, pull to shove,
Out to in, up to down, positive to negative,

Its rivers, its outbursts, its rain of fiery arches –
Their palpable elasticity; its arguments of plasma,

Furious conveyor belts, its pass-the-parcel,
Its trapped multitudes, local disturbances

Balancing and cancelling? Its points of stillness?

Flare

Body and Not Body. One figure of speech
Wrapped in another. Deep
Disagreement in its grammar.

One, serene on the surface, a furious
Circular argument, wrangling
Its implacable syntax.

The other, will o' the wisp
Skipping over the marshes,
Hovering above it, angelic presences,

Hotter by far, an incandescent
Ghost of itself, tearing its hair, ripping its skin,
Hoovering back, holding in, holding

In – until
It spills

Its body's intolerable secrets,
Guts and all.

Stolen Light

The lexicon scrabbles its alphabets.
Civility's nuts and bolts, rattling loose.

The violence of the marketplace, traders and thieves
Scattering their evidence.

Leaving their fingerprints.
Citrine. Cerise.

Who's stripped, walloped, identity stolen?
Who's mugged, bleeding green?

Who's this, tiptoeing, fleet, insignificant,
Through the hot mingle-pot, deft as a pick-pocket?

Corona

What do you mean, to be a thousand times hotter
Than the visible surface?

A strangeness, peculiar.
Will it respond to interrogation?

Calcium, iron, battered beyond recognition.
Will it confess

Insupportable temperature? Damage
Made legible? Does it disguise

Multiple identities? Are its fingerprints
Scanned in transit at the checkpoint?

Does it cross borders with impunity? What is
Its state, its port of origin, its language,

Its history of insurgency, what is it missing
In exile, is it explicable, does it

Constantly swap exotic
Bodies with itself, is it mythical, is it tenable,

What will hold onto it, how much reality
Is lost in translation?

Spicules

What is exciting you, little spikes?
Burning prairies at the Sun's edge,

Swaying grasses, fiery red,
Bristling jets, shooting up in bunches;
Visible envoys of invisible structure:

What are you saying, about density, about temperature,
Electromagnetics, Hydrodynamics –

Language and meaning –
How they talk to each other

In the space between what happens and what appears?

Null Point

Woosh! A sudden
Influx, spiralling down. Where
Will you dump yourself? Here!

In one alias or another:
Insupportable light.
Sound made visible.

A god, stamping its foot.
Hotting up the chromosphere.

Even
Here, hot, hottest, madly dynamic,
Everything is wedded to its opposite.

Loops, fiery wires, urgent to reconnect.

Even
Here, there will be such moments

When equal and opposite meet,
Cancel out,
And something opens,

Star-shaped and silent –

Where you are to be found,
Zero: the nothing that makes
Everything happen.

Magnetic Reconnection

You, Instigator –
Mischievous provocateur of drama –
Attraction, repulsion, disguise – what

Have you let us all in for?
Concealing yourself in the old garments,
Myth, metamorphosis – slippery as a river

Twisting a channel twisting
A river, question and answer
Spiralling about each other, a circular

Argument of sense and grammar

Which, stretched, snaps horribly
Apart, and horribly
Inseparable, language and thought

Spring immediately back
Into each other's palpable
Relief. The invisible

Rearranges itself. Slowly,
The ghostly, insensible presences
Appear.

The Sun makes a noise!

The whole Sun – its honeycomb,
Its pomegranate, its brilliant, seething layers –
Awash with its choirs

Has no truck with your language.

Smuggles its secrets in plain sight,
Broad daylight:
My countless tremors, my many, my One Pulse.

Pulse. Five minutes apart. Sense,
Out of its league, never built for this scale –
No grip on the implacable –

Grapples for images. Demands translation
From the odd oblique
Clue, such as this:

Sneaked "sound" leaves its fingerprints,
A wobble in the signature, the sequence
Of stolen light, inscribed by its elements.

Fraunhofer Lines

It plays like this:

Music, poured out
In silence, sequenced
Note by note –

Bent light, splayed,
Graceful, continuous
As a movie, sliced up

Frame by frame.
It radiates
From hot to cool.

Each hungry element
Steals from it,
Precise as a scale.

Window

Something crept in through a window
And set the factories to work

Processing their simple chemistry.
Something squeezed in

Through a crack, until what it made happen
Recognised it, and responded.

Something sneaked in with a message: imagine
Hydrogen crushed to metal. Iron

Maddened into gas, gas gone insane.
A small ship, its hatches battened.

Through the narrowest gap, something extends
A tentative question.

Frequencies

How does the Sun flow?
Its secrets
Darker than an ocean's strangeness.

Let the waves tell us.

Each an explorer,
Tasting its own precise

Level; speeded or slowed
By the hazards it endures.

No journey was ever so extreme.

And not one traveller
Returns unchanged. Each time,

It brings back its unique
Report, exact as light.

III

Various Uncertainties

II

Forget, warm body –
Forget the loud sea's
Boom and shudder;

Forget, strong weather,
Gust after gust –
You are only rumours:

Something broadcast
On a channel almost
Nobody listens to.

It is elsewhere, the party;
The ghostly
Immaterial numbers

Dancing all night
In the mirrored ballroom,

Or gazing transfixed
At their own beauty.

Speakable and Unspeakable

Words as labels, words as models:
Whichever you choose,
It is impossible

To speak a truth without contradiction.

For something to exist –
For anything to happen –
Something must pick a direction.

Symmetry must be broken.

But symmetry cannot be broken.
It is still there, hiding
In the merciless equations.

EDGE

First Rising Tide

Mare Anguis
Mare Ingenii
Mare Fecunditatis
Mare Imbrium
Mare Tranquillitatis
Oceanus Procellarum
Mare Undarum
Mare Marginis

Then like a wind on a dark river
Curling back and folding over,
Like the babble of its bubbles
In its streamers, froth and spirals,
Like a shockwave to a pebble
Or a raindrop to its ripples
Or a splash of milk in water,
Like a tree of branching numbers,
Like the frost unfurling flowers,
Like a loop between two mirrors –
Folding back and curling over
Like a wind on a dark river,

Everything there was, was flow –
A vast turbulence, in its interstices
Moments of rejection, making eddies, patterns –

Time's sieve
Sifting its dust.

The needle prick of an eye
Pinning its Now
On the black immensities.

Then out of their harmonic
Relation, into motion,
Summon into orbit
Star, moon, planet;
Like the anvil and the hammer
Or the strings that hum together,
Like the compass and the measure,
Into place and pattern
Time and explication,
Call them into music –

Now. Here.

Mare Anguis
Mare Ingenii
Mare Fecunditatis
Mare Imbrium

Mare Tranquillitatis
Oceanus Procellarum
Mare Undarum
Mare Marginis

Io

First postcard

I

Whatever it is that is making itself,
It is not finished.

Cankers, oozes, ulcers, itches.

Someone has scratched
A wound,

Flung open a furnace
A long way down, its black slag terraces
Glistening, the heat ferocious:

Glass, spluttering in a crucible.
Choking. Throwing up fistfuls of vitriol.
The glowing gathers dripping like honey.

Rich yolk-yellow vitreous enamel
Gorgeous ornament
Glinting, malignant.

Stitching and gashing itself,
Time's mirror,
Making and unmaking, unfinished.

II

A far-away machine.
Strange glazes,
Smoking in the kiln.

Lamps. Vapours.
Stink. Stythe. Stour.
A wound that heals itself over and over,

A skylight straight down.
A single eye,
Glowing. Gigantic.

Not far enough away.

Io, Jupiter's Moon

An immense beast
In harness.
An engine. A windless

Winding it in, drag-
Ging it
Out of shape; tug-

Ging and stretch-   *An engine.*
Ing it.
Downstream,

The invisible river   *A windless.*
Quickening,
                                           Green flame-sheets
A blindness
                                           Billowing.
Murmuring to itself;
Inside its whisper,
The unseen whirlpool's

Boom and thunder.

Enceladus

First postcard

I

Little sinister
Tinkles. Silvery
Trickles, tiny splinters –

Grit, salt, glass –
Dry, broken bits
Spit and splutter.

A gleam inside the dark inside
A mirror.

A note pitched way too high,
Zinging across an ice-sheet's
Ridge and furrow. Under it

A rumble. A mutter.
A tin sheet, shaken.

II

Ditches. Fissures. Iron
Miles. Scarps, folds.
Not rock. Ice,

Split. Canyons filled
With smashed walls, old
Darkness. Frost.

A locked fist of ice,
Wriggling inside it
A furious secret.

Water, arguing with itself.

What am I? What will I become?
Where next?

Enceladus, Saturn's Moon

What is more still than a little orb
Hung
From its hook

On Nothing?

Each orb, an exact
Pitch struck.

Pinned in place
By a silence.

Existing
Only in relation.

A chord.
A song.

What is more perfect?

A lens
Melding the various wavelengths of light,
Splinters of time.

Beyond it, the black silences

Un-answering.

Titan

First postcard

I

Slippery, equivocal. Circles
Within circles. A bubble.
Inside it, an engine:

The wheel that drags the ocean –
Caustic, pungent –
Up from its ice-prison,

Slopping, babbling
Through its lid of silence:

Here I am,
My own twin, twisting
Out of my stillness.

II

Slowly the rain falls, drop
By drop,

Splashing dry
Pebbles. A tawny

Twilit gloom.   *Drop*
Deep cold. A film   *By drop,*

Slowed right down.
Rain's soft percussion –
                                       Brown
Each drop
Full as a grape –
                                       Brine.
Falls like ash,   *Strewn*
Too far to hear.
                                       Stone.
Something idling
In the rain
                                       A cigarette-
Might discover   *Smoke brown*
It had begun

Dreaming itself   *Brine*
Out of sleep,
                                       Of gas,
On the cusp
Of nothingness.
                                       Cold, cold,
It might be this.

Something shimmering   *Stinking*

79

Out of time

Into sleep's
Oblivion,

Snuffed out just
As it begins:

A yellow slick.
A smear of rain.

A scattering
Of parched stone –

Ground, grooved,
Gouged, strewn

With smooth round
Tumbled gravel –

Juggled, ravelled,
Jumbled shingle –

A memory.

Once was a river.

Of ammonia,

Petroleum,
Engine-oil,

Bitter almonds.

Space Telescope

Infant, afloat in austere space,
Plump, dependent body tethered
By your tough umbilicus,
Face a mirror full of darkness;

Exquisite machine, your tinfoil
Wings, your booms' mosquito lightness,
Carrying our human hunger
Into the perpetual silence –

Intercede for us. The mountain
Cocks its ears, the wilderness
Of holy madmen strains to listen
For a song beyond extinction.

First High Tide

Mare Ingenii
Mare Vaporum
Mare Spumans
Mare Undarum

Somewhere the idea of spinning   *Sinus Amoris*
Into nothing, out of nothing,   *Sinus Asperitatis*

Inside out about its axis,   *Palus Somni*
Vortex curving into vortex,   *Sinus Fidei*

Proves the burning worlds, the oceans,   *Mare Ingenii*
Galaxies and star-fields, wormholes   *Mare Vaporum*

To this thought – a contradiction   *Mare Spumans*
Perfected by its imperfection.   *Mare Undarum*

Io

First falling tide

I

Not a miracle of clockwork.
Not the choreography and music
Of the spheres.

A ball of tumult.

Screams, gasps, grunts, howls, shrieks
Bending the dark,
Dragging back darkness like a catapult.

Glowing breakers
Leap, lunge – burst
Out of their dull black skin.

II

A fountainhead, a pulse, an issue
Of liquid, a fiery skein, a spitting
Cauldron of metal,

A whole round vitreous
Yellow world, twisting
Inside itself out, splitting

And mending itself, mad
For escape, where
Will I go, what will I

Become?

III

Hot, viscous orange,
A rubbery thick skin
Endlessly bursting

And stitching, a whole
History, wringing its hands,
Flexing its tenses –

Now, Then, Will Be, Was – spilling
And swallowing itself,
Forgetting

And forgetting.

First Falling Tide

Somewhere the idea of spinning
Into nothing, out of nothing,
Inside out about its axis,
Vortex curving into vortex,
Proves the burning worlds, the oceans,
Galaxies and star-fields, wormholes
To this thought – a contradiction
Perfected by its imperfection.

Like a wind on a dark river
Curling back and folding over,
Like the babble of its bubbles
In its streamers, froth and spirals,
Like the anvil and the hammer
Or the strings that hum together
Or a tree of branching numbers,
Like a loop between two mirrors –
Folding back and curling over
Like a wind on a dark river.

Enceladus

First falling tide

Not the singing anvil. Not the bell.
Not the pebble
Falling, ripples spreading.

Inside its inflexible incarnation of ice,
Water
Slops, sighs, a blue-green promise.

Where next?

Here!
Shot

Hundreds of miles
Into empty space.
Ice.

Ice, rippling like flames.
Ice as grains.
Ice in towering, toppling plumes,

Faster than a bullet,
Boiling and snowing at the same time.
How does the water

Under its ice-lid,
Thudding; straining
Its shoulder against a dead

How does the water
Under its ice-lid,
Thudding; straining

Weight; breathing
Its salt self, moving
In secret within itself,

Quarrelsome,
Troublesome,

Knotting

And unknotting, a strange
Amniotic dream,
An underground ocean,

Come

To be here? To pierce
Its prison of ice –

The claw-marks, the fractures,
The pressures, the heat –

To become

And keep on becoming?

Its shoulder against a dead
Weight; breathing
Its salt self, moving

In secret within itself,
Quarrelsome,
Troublesome;

The claw-marks, the fractures,
The pressures, the heat –

Second Rising Tide

In this tide's heave, everything becomes an ocean
Flowing, provisional: names, inventions, mountains, even
Whole round worlds, on their way to elsewhere –

Every one of them an element in darkness,
A spark, a spelk, a splinter of something endless,

A fluency, imagining itself imagining
Some solid architecture – endlessly twisting
Inside it, its own fluid selves, its almost-ruin.

Io

Second rising tide

I

A gust. A gliff. Hot glass, stotting on frost.
A tinkle of broken bits. Quiet. A whisper.

Matter's baby-cries.
Little sobs and whimpers.

Fizz. Sizzle. Spit.
Cinders

Sifting themselves in the grate.
Dross. Embers.

If somebody was to invent a god it would sound like this.

An infant.
An absolute potentate.

Then out of the forge,
Out of the pot of light, heat – heaving, deep at its root –
A spasm,
A sluice,   *A spasm,*
A rush,   *A sluice,*
A hot foul hiss,   *A rush,*
A flood,   *A hot foul hiss,*
An appalling torrent –   *A flood;*
An incandescent wall of unmade matter
Boiling over – all

Gods, prayers, images, languages, shrieks

Gods, prayers, images,
Languages, shrieks —

Superfluous. Look –

I am World, uttering myself.

II

Gas becoming metal. Metal
Becoming liquid.
Everywhere, the imperative

To be elsewhere. Waves
Within waves, quick, slow,
Trying out their tenses –

Here, Now – swell
And counterswell, a terrible
Undertow dragging them

Apart, inside it
Something blacker than absolute
Zero. Light's negative.

Resisting it,
This one tremendous, opposite
Impulsion:

Flow.

Titan

Second rising tide

Wind becoming ocean.
Wave-scribbled dunes.

Gullies. Long meanders.
The memory of rivers.

Salt crusts at the corner
Of the lake's eye.

A freeze-dried stream-bed.
Nothing. Nothing. Then

A stew,
A broth,
A muck-sweat,
A brew,
Cold spluttering stock,
Cold orange glow,
Lees, scum,
Froth, foul
Exhalations,
A film of oil,
All the colours of light squirming inside it.

Out of the stuff of stars –
Gas, dust, ice –
Someone is painstakingly

Threading a necklace.

A river, braiding its bitter

Currents, turning its beads
Over and over,

Showing them to the dim
Yellow dusk, to storm-cloud
Hem, seam, worrying

And fumbling, its meaningless
Muttering to itself
Repeating itself, until

The thread snaps. Beads
Spill. Roll. A scattering.
Whose

Dim eyes, amnesiac fingers,
Begin again,
Blindly restringing them?

This chemical spiritous
River that sings
Of nothing but itself.

Highest Tide

Like the strings that hum together,
Like a loop between two mirrors
Folding back and curling over
Like a wind on a dark river...

Sinus Amoris
Sinus Asperitatis
Palus Somni
Sinus Fidei

Moon

I

Too long in the oven, a grey cinder.
A pumice-stone. A lump of clinker.

Snowshine grit, asbestos desert,
Its daylight sky as black as velvet,

Knife-edge salt-ridge building site,
A cold dead ash-can, emptied out,

White-out stone-yard. Nothing's mirror,
Stripped of sound, leeched of colour.

Fossil footprints. In the distance
The tremor from some random violence.

Scrapyard. Relic. Extinct war-zone,
Blasted. Battered. Uproar frozen

Ever-after, moments smashed
Into grains of powdered glass

Stacked up in their billions,
Fixed in a snapshot's flinty brilliance –

A stillness, exquisitely balanced
On the needle of this silence.

II

A door
Opening on a silence

On another silence. In the dust
An ancient inscription.

A memory
Etched upon a memory.

Frozen. An ocean's heave –
Monumental waves –
These rippling mountains;

Beyond them, a lost script,
Reticulate
Texture of noughts, a cipher

Inscribed over

And over, an endless   *Mare Anguis*
Incontrovertible record, endurance   *Mare Ingenii*

Beyond wounds, howls, sounds, beyond   *Mare Fecunditatis*
Pain, beyond   *Mare Imbrium*
Everything, a document   *Mare Tranquillitatis*

Containing a darkness   *Oceanus Procellarum*
That has never seen sunlight –   *Mare Undarum*
So old, so deep, so cold and permanent   *Mare Marginis*

You dare not drill into it.

III

Moon stared out into a blackness
Blacker than the inside of ink.
It bent the dark around it like a question.

The sky pulled inside out.
No down or up.
Nothing's sluice ajar,
Its dark flood roaring in.

Such a small blue boat,
Its hull exquisite glass,
Eggshell-delicate,
A bowl of turquoise light

Afloat in that deep dark:
This one blue eye
Aglow. Alight
From the inside out.

IV

Moon could not look away.
It tugged at its anchor.
The eye stared back. There was nothing to see.

Far away, a lens. Light, bending.
A pattern of dark and bright transparencies,

Strings breaking

And mending,

Copying. Recopying.
The water a mirror.
One wave, coiling around another.

Smashed glass. Slag. Ash.
The stoved-in dark dragged the water into it
As if it was breathing. In and out.

Here and gone.

V

The Moon had made it:
One blue mote, afloat in a voracious
Stream inside a stream inside a current, inside it

A loop
Twisting itself
Through a figure eight;

An urgency
Seeking a body
Wanting to be free of a body;

A wave
Endlessly chasing and devouring
Its own shadow;

A dark
Understanding itself
Through a needle's eye.

CODA

Wake

Trinity Hall, Cambridge

Where are you off to? High walls crooked around you,
Porters, polishers, stirrers of pots, the unseen
Choreography of the household; behind you

Spike-rush, feathery reed,
Dragonfly, mosquito-cloud – Fen
Clay, clunch and oolite, at its root, a faint scent of the sea.

Wake up, says the moon,

Looming crescent over cupola and weather-vane,
Sediments of ancient limestone –
Desolate, implacable – It's me,

Unmaking, remaking myself in an endless circle,
Suspended above your incomprehensible puzzle
Like judgement, or mercy.

An Education

For the Institute for Computational Cosmology

Durham, black-veined, coal-seamed, your House of God
Frosted with fossil sea-lilies – inside the noose
Your river has twisted, supple as plasticine,

Our young minds grappled with the Incarnation.
Unfathomable as the paradox of time and distance,
The haul of radio-telescopes, trawling the darkness.

Why did nobody tell us?
The equation of energy and mass could better explain
The mysteries of origin. The patient machines

Whirring for weeks, would map each filament,
Plot and predict the dark, its exact distribution
Precise as the sea-floor highways of the brain,

Lighting them up like cities at night
Glimpsed from space, as the lights begin to go out.

Intertidal

Beadnell, 2015

I walked out to the end of the Broad Rock
At low spring tide. A prehistoric
Foreshore, empty pavement, jagged, violent

Brown stone, broken apart under the sky's
Hammer. Strange shrieks. Wild shouts loosed from somewhere

Very far away – vast, wide, metallic,
Mineral. In every seam and channel,
Slippery, smelling briny with excitement –

Beards, groins, armpits, dripping pelts
The colours of old bronze, dried blood, new grass –

Carrageen, corallina, sea-oak, saw-wrack,
Unpicking the chemistry of air, salt water, sunlight.

Before me, kelp beds, freshly-exposed; then the sea's glitter –
Green algae, gobbling the red gleam close to the surface.
Red algae, eating the blue gloom in the deep water.

The tawny, the ochre, leathery, rubbery, feathery –
Floating, provisional, shuffling their elements,

As far as light can penetrate, until
There is nothing here but process.

And I have to turn back.

NOTES

These notes are intended only to provide background to the poems. Writing these poems has shown me how, like poetry, the beauty of science often reveals ever-deeper levels of complexity, and a statement that might be "true" at a simple level might not be so at a deeper one. Any misunderstandings are of course my own. More accurate explanations of the science can be found by following the italicised terms on Wikipedia.

I

P.29: This first poem of *Field* introduces several of the key ideas in the sequence. *Quantum physics* describes the behaviour of *subatomic particles*, the building blocks of the Universe. Quantum fluctuations were amplified by the rapid expansion of the early Universe from an initial singularity in what is known as the Big Bang, which created space and time. Both quantum mechanics and the fundamental forces of nature are described by *fields*, which can be thought of as the assignment of a physical quantity at each point of space and time. While quantum physics describes interactions at a subatomic scale, *General Relativity* describes the cosmic-scale geometry of gravity, space and time. However, these two theories, spectacularly accurate in their own spheres, are incompatible: the very small and the very large 'will not mesh'. *Gravitational decoherence* is the mechanism by which the quantum coherence of a particle is diminished due to its interaction with the gravitational field.

Pp.30-31: In the *Standard Model* of particle physics, the *Higgs mechanism* is essential to explain how a particular class of particles have the property of *mass*. The Higgs field has a symmetry that is broken below an extremely high temperature. This is known as *spontaneous symmetry breaking* and gives rise to the masses of particles. Without it, matter could not coalesce, and the Universe could not form.

Pp.32-33: *Gravity* is the phenomenon by which all things with mass or energy are pulled towards one another. General Relativity describes it as a consequence of the curvature of space-time, caused

111

by the uneven distribution of mass. Without it, the Universe would have no objects and no structure. The most extreme example of this curvature of space-time is a black hole, from which, beyond a certain event horizon (according to the simplest description), nothing, not even light, can escape. Although the dominant force in the Universe at the cosmic scale, gravity has a far less significant influence at a subatomic scale. Current researchers seek to develop a theory of gravity consistent with quantum mechanics (a *Theory of Everything*), but at present many unanswered questions remain. Unlike other forces, gravity's force-carrying particle, the graviton, has not been directly detected. Gravitational effects suggest that the Universe contains about 85% unobservable *dark matter*. While gravity pulls the Universe together, what is the nature of the phenomenon known as *dark energy* which appears to be pulling it apart at an ever-faster rate? The young science of Cosmology addresses such questions.

P.34: *Symmetries* are properties of the Universe which form a key part of *Field Theory*. According to the Standard Model, the fundamental *forces* of nature (such as electromagnetism) can be explained by them. Forces are transmitted by particles called *gauge bosons*. The fundamental fields from which forces are derived cannot be directly measured, but their associated quantities can be. Different configurations of unobservable fields can result in identical observations. A transformation from one to another is known as a *gauge transformation*. When no change occurs in the measurable quantities when a field is transformed, that is known as *gauge symmetry* or *gauge invariance*. All fundamental interactions arise from the constraints of *local* gauge symmetries. This poem plays with the idea of the symmetries of the Universe, their locally-observed constraints contained within the brackets of an equation.

P.35: *Electromagnetic radiation* from an early stage of the Universe pervades all space. Sensitive radio telescopes show a faint background glow, the *cosmic microwave background*. This is considered extremely important evidence for the Big Bang theory of the origin of the Universe. It is thought that the early Universe was filled with a uniform white-hot fog of hydrogen plasma. As it expanded and cooled, protons and electrons combined to form hydrogen atoms, and the Universe became transparent, allowing *photons* (the electromagnetic particle) to travel freely through space. The cosmic microwave background is the relic of that first visible radiation; nearly, but not quite, uniform. (As the Universe expanded, these tiny initial irregularities were magnified, and they help to explain the structure of the Universe we see today.) This poem celebrates that "first light", and the 'exquisite accident' of the evolution of an 'instrument' to interpret it – an 'infant' species, currently occupying the third rock from the Sun.

P.36: This poem revisits the *phase transition* which is thought to have occurred fractions of a second after the Big Bang, as the ultra-hot Universe cooled, triggering the spontaneous symmetry breaking of the *Higgs mechanism*.

P.37: Like all fundamental fields, the *Higgs field* exists throughout space. As we have seen, it has a symmetry which is broken. Its interaction with the electromagnetic field gives particles their characteristic properties. This explains how the gauge bosons of the weak force, W and Z, become massive at all temperatures below an extremely high value. The same field also explains, in a different way, why other fundamental particles have mass. The Higgs field was likened by Professor David Miller of University College London to a crowded cocktail party. A celebrity trying to move through the crowd is slowed down, in the way that the Higgs field gives mass to a particle. Although scientists at CERN succeeded in identifying the *Higgs boson*, the particle associated with the Higgs field, many questions remain – in particular, the reason for the mass of the Higgs boson itself. This poem introduces the idea of *supersymmetry*, an extension of the Standard Model which aims to fill some of these gaps. An alternative theory is that of the *multiverse*, which some theorists favour to explain the value of the Higgs mass.

Pp.38-39: There are two classes of elementary particle, *fermions*, the basic building blocks of matter, and *bosons*, some of which are responsible for transmitting force. Elementary particles, composite particles (hadrons) and atomic nuclei carry an intrinsic form of *angular momentum*, called *spin*. The poem grapples with this difficult concept, referring to the fact that bosons have integer spin and fermions half-integer. These qualities determine how the particles combine either to mediate force, or to make matter (the spin of electrons in turn underlies the periodic table of chemical elements). This poem also refers to the *Pauli Exclusion Principle*, which states that fermions cannot be in the same place at the same time with the same energy. That is not true of bosons, which 'stack up in heaps'. The Higgs boson has *zero spin*.

P.40: Space is a vacuum but contains a multiplicity of fields, with every point of space and time assigned a physical quantity. This includes the Higgs field which, as we have seen, interacts with most classes of particle to give them mass. There are exceptions, which include two gauge bosons which are not given mass by the Higgs: the *photon* (carrier of electromagnetism) and the *gluon* (carrier of the strong force).

P.41: This poem returns to some of the as-yet unanswered questions of our Universe: its missing mass (*dark matter*), accelerating expansion (*dark energy*), and the theory of supersymmetry introduced earlier. It also touches on the hypothetical multiverse and, in particular, *string theory*, a theory of quantum gravity in which point-like particles are replaced by one-dimensional vibrating strings. In this and related theories, a *brane* is a physical, dynamic object that can propagate through space-time, generalising a point to higher dimensions.

P.42: The final poem of the sequence returns to the dominant idea of symmetry breaking by the Higgs mechanism initiating the processes from which our Universe was created and by which it continues to unfold. The poem concludes with a metaphor to show that the Universe as we know it – space, time, matter and force – exists, as if in a dream-state, in relation to the symmetries and pure energy of the Big Bang.

II

P.45: An *aurora* is a display of light close to the poles of a planet or moon that has a strong magnetic field and an atmosphere. It is caused by charged particles from the solar wind accelerating along that planet's magnetic field and interacting with a gas in its atmosphere. On Earth, auroras are seen at high latitudes, as charged particles from the Sun disturb Earth's magnetosphere, exciting oxygen and nitrogen in the atmosphere which, as it returns to its usual state, emits light of various colours. The Northern Lights, sometimes visible from the UK, are often a greenish hue due to oxygen. Auroras appear on other planets and moons in the solar system, but on Earth they help remind us of the highly unusual conditions which have made it possible for life to evolve: first, the Sun's heat and light; secondly, Earth's magnetic field, which protects us from the most damaging effects of solar radiation; and thirdly Earth's atmosphere, which further filters out much of the Sun's dangerous UV light.

P.46: Scientists examining the Sun study the radiation released at its surface, which covers a wide range of wavelengths across the electromagnetic spectrum, from radio waves to X-rays and gamma rays. It is dangerous to look directly at the Sun, but special solar telescopes, both on Earth and in space, can safely "see" far beyond the visible. By examining different types of radiation, it is possible to view different layers of the Sun's atmosphere, and different processes and structures within it. These investigations reveal the Sun to be extremely dynamic. NASA's Solar Dynamics Observatory (SDO) photographs the Sun in 10 different wavelengths. Extreme ultraviolet photographic images, taken at 30.4nm (for the chromosphere) and at shorter wavelengths (for the corona) are reproduced on the SDO's website in different colours. The "green" coronal channel images from the ESA-NASA Solar and Heliospheric Observatory (SOHO) inspired this poem. It reflects on how little of the reality of the physical Universe is immediately available to our senses, which have evolved to cope only with conditions on Earth.

Pp.48-64: The poems in this sequence investigate the methods which solar scientists use to look inside the Sun and to examine its structure and processes in more detail. From these methods we know that the Sun is made up of several layers. At its *core*, enormous densities and temperatures (15 million degrees C) provide conditions for the nuclear fusion reactions which power it, converting hydrogen to helium. Energy is then radiated outwards by photons which are absorbed and re-emitted randomly by atoms in the *radiative zone*. Moving further away from the core, as temperatures cool, convection takes over. In the *convection zone* warmer material rises and is replaced by cooler material descending from above. This upwelling of hot material and sinking of cooler material gives the *photosphere*, the Sun's visible surface, its granular appearance. Beyond the photosphere, in the *chromosphere*, hydrogen atoms absorb energy from the photosphere and re-emit it as reddish light. Beyond this chromosphere stretches the Sun's outer atmosphere, its *corona*. The layer between the chromosphere and corona rises steeply in temperature and is called the "Transition Region". *Solar prominences*, which have temperatures similar to that of the chromosphere, hang in the corona supported by the Sun's magnetic field. *Solar flares*, which are releases of unimaginably huge amounts of energy, erupt from the Sun's atmosphere. The poems which follow explore some of the science behind these findings.

P.48: This poem was inspired by a *magnetogram* image, taken by the Michelson Doppler Imager on SOHO. These images are reproduced by convention in grey, black and white, and show the strength and location of the Sun's magnetic field. The image I was looking at suggested a relatively quiet surface, but very different images of the Sun's atmosphere at various wavelengths from other instruments aboard SOHO show its exquisite structures and violently dynamic processes. A palimpsest of images suggests that the Sun has many simultaneous faces, depending on the instrument examining it, the wavelength at which it is examined, and the temperature under examination.

P.49: The Sun is a giant ball of *plasma*, large enough to hold more than a million Earths inside it, and consisting mainly of hydrogen and helium. This electrically-charged plasma continually circulates, generating an enormous magnetic field. It works as a gigantic *dynamo*. The Sun's fluid structure allows its rotation to vary with latitude, which causes its magnetic field to become increasingly twisted over time. This distorted field increases and diminishes over an 11-year cycle. Professor Valentina Zharkova (Northumbria University) has presented an important new model of the Sun's 11-year cycle, showing irregularities in its "heartbeat", caused by a *double dynamo* effect in two layers of the Sun, one close to its surface and the other deep within the convection zone.

P.50: Patches of the Sun's surface oscillate up and down at regular five-minute intervals, due to sound (pressure) waves which are generated and trapped within the convection zone. *Helioseismologists* use these waves, and the *modes* of vibration which they produce, to "look" inside the Sun in the same way that geologists use seismic waves from earthquakes to look inside the Earth. The properties of these waves help them determine the temperature, density, composition and motion of the Sun's interior. Although the Sun is highly dynamic and violent over periods of days and years, in the long term it is immensely stable at this stage of its billions-of-years-long life-cycle, because its tremendous gravity is balanced by its enormous internal pressure. This balance is known as *hydrostatic equilibrium*.

P.51: This poem refers to the Sun's differential *rotation patterns* which play a role in generating its magnetic fields. We know about these because of the sound waves generated in the convection zone, which move into and back out of the Sun at various depths. Some waves travel right through the centre of the Sun and can be used to examine its far side, identifying sunspots before they appear. This method can help to predict the electromagnetic activity which can result in solar flares and coronal mass ejections – activity which could potentially interfere with satellites in space and even affect Earth.

P.52: Using data from SOHO's Michelson Doppler Imager, Professor Zharkova has shown that a solar flare can send streams of charged particles crashing into the photosphere, creating a massive *sunquake* that ripples the Sun's surface. Film of this event on the Stanford University website inspired this poem: http://soi.stanford. edu/press/agu05-98/ Sunquakes are another tool by which Helioseismologists examine and predict the Sun's internal workings.

P.53: As the Sun's magnetic activity grows in its 11-year cycle, it breaks through the surface as visible *sunspots*. Sunspots are associated with enormous magnetic disturbances, such as solar flares, gigantic loops of magnetic field and plasma which burst from the Sun's surface and reconnect, throwing out X-rays into space and sending streams of charged particles crashing down onto the solar surface, causing sunquakes. This poem was inspired by astonishing film from SDO, showing glowing prominences and flares, which are detectable in extreme ultraviolet wavelengths invisible to the human eye. The sunspots which gather and fall away cyclically over 11 years are the visible signature of these gigantic electromagnetic loops and arches.

P.54: This poem attempts to relate different areas of solar physics into one coherent whole: the Sun's various layers, its dynamism and equilibrium, and ways of understanding it through its electromagnetic activity (*magnetohydrodynamics*) and seismic activity (*helioseismology*).

P.55: Another poem about different ways of "looking" at the Sun. It appears serene on its photosphere, but dramatic and unpredictable in its chromosphere and corona. The poem refers to the science of magnetohydrodynamics, the study of the magnetic properties and behaviour of electrically conducting fluids. It was inspired by reading about the relation between electric current and magnetic field in the Sun's plasma (highly-*ionised* gas). Unbound positive and negative particles move and generate electric current within a magnetic field, while any movement affects and is affected by fields created by other charges. Plasma trapped inside flux ropes rises up from the photosphere, in a tangle of electromagnetic loops and filaments which burst out in *solar flares*. The poem ends with a larger, more violent explosion called a *coronal mass ejection*, which throws billions of tonnes of the Sun's heated atmosphere into the solar system.

P.56: This poem explores the processes which reveal the Sun's chemical composition. The electrons surrounding an atomic nucleus are restricted to certain energy levels. When an energetic photon interacts with an atom, it may "kick" an electron to a higher energy level. This energised state is inherently unstable, so at some point the electron will fall back to a lower energy level, emitting a photon at a characteristic wavelength. Atoms higher up the periodic table have more electrons, so a wider range of "jumps" up and down energy levels is possible. The permissible jumps for a particular element form a unique "fingerprint", seen as *spectral lines*. There are two types of spectral line. One set, black *absorption lines*, are caused when photons are absorbed ('stolen') by the "up" jump.

The other set, *emission lines*, are bright lines of characteristic wave-length (colour) on the spectrum, caused by photons given off when the excited electron falls back to its lower energy state. Absorption lines dominate the photosphere's spectrum (see *Fraunhofer Lines*, p.62), while emission lines dominate the corona. The most prominent emission line in the chromosphere's spectrum is hydrogen alpha, in the red part of the spectrum, which gives the chromosphere its name (from *chroma*, meaning colour). Other bright emission lines from the chromosphere are those for helium. The chromosphere is hotter than the photosphere, and the corona much hotter again. The poem describes how, in the corona's highly-ionised plasma, many electrons are flying around free, stripped from their parent atoms. The corona emits the green "coronium" line, caused by the emission of photons from an iron ion that has lost 13 of its electrons.

P.57: As we have seen in the previous note, the *corona* consists of highly-ionised plasma. It is a thousand times hotter than the photosphere. Magnetic fields are responsible for this intense heating, but the exact mechanisms are mysterious, and the subject of much research in solar magnetohydrodynamics.

P.58: *Spicules* are dynamic jets in the chromosphere, associated with regions of high magnetic flux. They appear in photographs as 'burning prairies at the Sun's edge'. They are associated with a particular sort of low-frequency magnetohydrodynamic wave, the *Alfvén wave*. Their exact origin and effects are the subject of research within the solar magnetohydrodynamics community.

P.59: When the Sun's twisted magnetic field breaks under the strain, it releases a colossal amount of energy in a solar flare, in which the magnetic field rearranges itself into a lower energy state. Energy, which cannot be created or destroyed, only transformed, hides in the magnetic field. If the magnetic field is forced to move, it brings plasma with it. If plasma is forced to move, it brings the magnetic field with it. Collisions which break field lines sever this complicity, scattering charged particles, but the complicity immediately reconfigures itself in a lower energy state. This poem pictures electrons spiralling down field lines from the corona, dumping their energy in the chromosphere as heat or sound. Magnetic field lines always appear in pairs – a source and a sink. However, within the corona there are magnetic *null points* where the field is zero. Fast wave energy accumulates close to these null points, and they become locations of preferential heating by a particular type of wave. Although this effect is local, it provides a vital clue to why the corona is so much hotter than the photosphere.

P.60: The snapping of twisted magnetic field in a solar flare is known as *magnetic reconnection*. In the Sun, plasma cannot move without shifting the magnetic field, and the magnetic field will not allow the plasma to escape. Magnetic reconnection is a process occurring in all layers of the Sun, in which the magnetic topology is rearranged and magnetic energy is converted into heat and kinetic energy. The SDO has recorded astonishing video of solar flares in which these processes are made visible. Watching them on the SDO website inspired the imagery of this poem.

P.61: This poem returns to Helioseismology. As we have seen, the Sun's oscillations are principally caused by sound waves generated and trapped within the convection zone. These combine into resonant *modes*. Global oscillations are visible as a pulse with a period of about five minutes. A wave of a certain frequency travels into the Sun into a subsurface layer flowing at speed and, depending on whether it flows with or against the current, the frequency of the wave is affected, speeded up or slowed down. A type of frequency splitting provides a way of measuring the flow velocities beneath the surface. Travelling sound waves mapped in this way show that the interior of the Sun rotates very differently from the surface.

P.62: *Fraunhofer lines* are dark lines in the Sun's electromagnetic spectrum, caused by absorption of the Sun's radiation at specific wavelengths by chemical elements in the solar atmosphere. This "barcode" reveals the complete chemical composition of the Sun (see note for p.56).

P.63: This is a poem about the influence of the Sun on the Earth. The Sun is essential to life, but also has the potential to destroy it. Earth, at a perfect distance from the Sun, is protected from the most damaging effects of "solar wind" by its magnetic field, which acts as a barrier to deflect particles and radiation. Earth's atmosphere further filters out much of the dangerous UV part of the spectrum, allowing through just enough heat and light to spark and nurture life.

P.64: A concluding poem about helioseismology, in which sound waves are used to "look" inside and to the far side of the Sun, which enables scientists to examine its structure and to predict solar activity.

III

Pp.70-100: The structure of *Edge* is based on "fly-bys" of four moons in our solar system. Each fly-by is at a different distance, and each moon represents one of the four "primal elements" identified by the Ancient Greeks. The piece visits and revisits each of the first three moons, as a tide might reveal, and then cover it again. The poem ends at Earth's own Moon. The idea of *tides* is important in astronomy, describing the gravitational effects which stretch and squeeze the first three of these moons, while our Moon exerts its own gravitational tidal effect upon water on Earth.

Pp.70-71, 82, 95, 97: The chant is mostly composed of the names of *lunar maria*, the so-called "seas" on Earth's Moon. Science shows these to be large plains of dark basalt rock, resulting from long-ago volcanic eruptions or ancient impacts. Early astronomers believed these dark areas to be actual seas, and also identified some locations as "sinus" (bay) or "palus" (marsh). These names occur later in the chant.

Pp.72-74, 83-85, 90-91: *Io*, one of Jupiter's four large moons, is the most volcanic body in the solar system. Its violent activity is due to the intense heat generated by tidal squeezing and stretching, caused by its elliptical orbit around the gas giant and the gravitational influence of Jupiter's other large moons. Io is one of the most terrifying and inhospitable places imaginable. It has the fewest water molecules of any known body in the solar system. Its active volcanoes spew out plumes of sulphur and sulphur dioxide that rise 300 miles above its surface, and most of that surface is covered in a frost of those chemicals which colour it yellow, red, white, black and green. From 1995 to 2003 NASA's Galileo spacecraft revealed giant lava flows, lava lakes and enormous, collapsing mountains, higher than Mount Everest. It also discovered a belt of high-energy radiation centred on Io's orbit. Photographs from that mission inspired these sections of the poem. To find a language to write about it, I drew upon some extreme processes from heavy industry. 'Stythe' is a word used by Durham miners to describe toxic gases and 'stour' is a northern word meaning dust.

P.92: The lines in this intermediate section, moving away from Io, refer first to the high-energy radiation centred on the moon's orbit, then to *dark energy*, the mysterious force pushing the universe apart at an ever-faster rate, against the pull of gravity. The paradox 'blacker than absolute zero' was inspired by a précis of an article from the journal *Science* in January 2013. Classic thermodynamic systems cannot achieve temperatures below absolute zero (-273.15 degrees C). But in the article, quantum physicists reported the creation in the laboratory of an atomic gas that could attain a negative temperature. According to that report, the sub-absolute zero gas mimicked dark energy – an idea which found its way into *Edge*.

Pp.75-77, 87-88: *Enceladus*, a tiny moon of Saturn, intrigued scientists because, in spite of being so far from the Sun, it is extremely bright. NASA's Cassini mission (1997-2017) began studying Enceladus in 2005, and solved the mystery of why it is the most reflective object in the solar system. Astonishing photographs from that mission inspired these sections of the poem. The text on p.77, based on a photograph, observes Enceladus from afar, held by the delicate harmonies of Saturn's gravity, apparently, as was once believed, 'still' and 'perfect'. But Cassini proved otherwise. First, its scientists discovered that Enceladus's icy surface is covered in crevasses, faults, ridges and ice boulders the size of houses, showing that it is young and active. This was consistent with the constantly changing gravitational forces of its elliptical orbit around Saturn, which stretch and squeeze it. However, mysterious *tiger stripes* near the south pole were unexpectedly revealed to be much warmer than the equator. Cassini's scientists discovered giant plumes of water vapour and ice erupting from these stripes, feeding Saturn's outer rings, and forming fresh, reflective ice on the surface of Enceladus, keeping it shiny white.

When I was writing *Edge*, this research was still in progress, and the poem alludes to its unanswered questions. There was much excitement in the scientific community at the time, because Cassini's scientists had discovered salt in the water from Enceladus's plumes, evidence that there was a liquid ocean beneath its south pole. More excitingly still, they had discovered that the water from the plumes contained organic materials, the building blocks of life on Earth. Peter and I chose to write about Enceladus for that reason.

It was not until two years after we finished *Edge*, however, in 2015, that two further astonishing discoveries were announced: first, a wobble in the moon's orbit shows that its ocean is not limited to its south pole but that its ice crust is floating on a global ocean. Secondly, methane and particles of silica in Enceladus's plumes led Cassini's scientists to conclude that its ocean is heated by *hydrothermal vents*. Hydrothermal vents in Earth's oceans are the foundation of rich ecosystems, cycling energy and nutrients up from the mantle. Life depends upon this flow and movement. Enceladus's plumes also contain molecular hydrogen, one of the food-sources for life on Earth. If there is life elsewhere in the solar system, Enceladus is indeed, as was suspected at the time I was writing this poem, a prime candidate.

Pp.78-80, 93-94: *Titan* is the largest moon of Saturn and the only one known to have a dense, nitrogen-rich atmosphere. In 2005 the NASA Cassini mission successfully landed ESA's Huygens probe on Titan, revealing a world that looked at first glance surprisingly Earth-like. Images from Cassini-Huygens provided inspiration for this part of the poem. They show vast, rippling hydrocarbon-rich dunes at Titan's equator and, at its poles, lakes and seas of methane and ethane. At the extremely cold temperatures of this world these substances are liquid, not gas, and play the role that water plays on Earth. Methane and ethane fall from Titan's clouds as rain, cycling this material back to the surface. Astonishing video from the descent of the Huygens probe onto Titan, available on the ESA website, shows branching networks of drainage channels and linear, canyon-like features carved by liquid methane. The landing site

123

itself resembles a dried-up river bed, covered in rounded pebbles, which are thought to be made up of hydrocarbons and water ice. Sound from the Huygens probe's descent provided raw data for Peter's music.

The Cassini-Huygens mission revealed that, deep below its surface, Titan harbours a large internal ocean of water and ammonia. The variety of chemicals observed in Titan's atmosphere indicates a rich and complex chemistry originating from methane and nitrogen and evolving into complex molecules, eventually forming the smog that surrounds the icy moon. Titan is very hostile: its atmosphere contains extremely toxic hydrogen cyanide, referred to in the poem by the smell of 'bitter almonds'. Numerous questions remain unanswered, but it is clear that, while very different from Enceladus, Titan shares with it many of the conditions necessary for life to evolve. In Titan's case, however, this would be a truly alien life-form. Rather than having water as its solvent, it would be methane-based, requiring an imaginative leap in how life is defined.

Pp.96-100: Half a century ago, in 1969, human beings set foot for the first time on the Moon. This part of the poem is inspired by my own childhood memories of those grainy images, together with contemporary written accounts, and sharply-detailed photographs from NASA's Apollo missions which show a dead and hostile world, covered with impact craters and ancient basalt lava "seas": 'magnificent desolation', as astronaut Buzz Aldrin described it.

Not long before I began writing *Edge*, NASA's unmanned Lunar Reconnaissance Orbiter had begun mapping the Moon. At its poles, it investigated craters in permanent shadow which have not seen sunlight for billions of years. After I had finished *Edge*, NASA confirmed that these craters contain hidden stores of water ice, which could one day enable human habitation. Part of the LRO's mission was to search for valuable resources, and the poem touches on the fact that space agencies and private companies were already beginning to talk about mining the Moon.

Among the most striking visual images from the 1960s-70s Apollo programme were those which showed views of Earth from the Moon. Astronauts reported feeling extremely moved by this view, recognising for the first time the beauty of Earth's exquisitely thin layer of blue atmosphere, and its true fragility. The end of *Edge* was inspired by those images and observations, together with scientific hypotheses about the relation of Earth to its Moon.

The Moon was probably formed out of the Earth itself, following a catastrophic impact about 4.5 billion years ago. Its gravitational influence significantly stabilises Earth's rotation, making our planet habitable. The Moon's gravitational pull is also responsible for most of the tidal movement of Earth's oceans. The intertidal area, a region of flow and refreshment, seems key to the evolution of life, particularly the lineages which colonised land and ultimately gave rise to humans. The origins of life on Earth, however, are less clear. If life originated around deep ocean hydrothermal vents, the Moon probably had little or no effect. The poem touches on another theory, which maintains that DNA and RNA molecules evolved in the intertidal area and that the fast tidal cycling of the early Earth due to the Moon's greater proximity aided their replication.

In the course of researching *Edge* I discovered that most scientists now agree that there may well be life elsewhere in our solar system – in which case life could be common across the Universe. But Earth remains the one place in the Universe that we know with certainty hosts conscious life. In the words of Carl Sagan, 'We are a way for the cosmos to know itself' (*Cosmos*, *episode 1*, 1990). We can only hope that the 'fossil footprints' from the Apollo mission will not outlast the species that created them.